JESUS CHRIST SOLID ROCK

The Return of Christ

David Wilkerson
with
Kathryn Kuhlman·Hal Lindsey
W.A.Criswell·Pat Boone

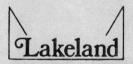

Lakeland

LAKELAND
116 BAKER STREET
LONDON W1M 2BB

First British Edition 1973

Scripture quotations indicated (MLB) in this book are taken from *The Modern Language Bible—The New Berkeley Version in Modern English*, © 1945, 1959, 1969 by the Zondervan Publishing House. Used by permission.

ISBN 0 551 00437 1

Printed in Great Britain
by J. W. Arrowsmith Ltd., Bristol

CONTENTS

WHAT IT'S ALL ABOUT

Jesus Christ . . . Solid Rock is a book for *thinking* youth. Dare to read it through, word for word! A power and spirit force beyond anything you have known will grip you.

Jesus Christ is now the only solid ground left in a sinking, dying world.

In the Bible, Jesus refers to believers as His "bride." While on earth He pinpointed a time in history He would return to "capture" His bride from the earth.

THAT HOUR HAS COME!

Any moment now — night or day — millions will suddenly disappear. It will happen in the twinkling of an eye — a split second. Every true Jesus person will vanish from the earth to meet Jesus Christ in the celestial heavens, leaving a shocked world behind! This is not a joke — it is not a fantasy — it is the absolute truth!

Jesus Christ is coming soon. He gave certain signs to prove His coming was "right at the door." The world has witnessed the *fulfillment of these signs.*

Read all about it in this unusual book.

This world is in its midnight hour — and who can honestly deny it? And so a cry is now being made: "Behold — Jesus Christ the Bridegroom is coming for His bride."

5

God predicted a Jesus restoration movement just before the end. That Spirit outpouring is right now sweeping the earth. It is the last sign — the last call — the last conviction. If you dare to read this book through, one of two things will happen:

1. Pride and secret sin will force you to deny and reject this truth *or*
2. You will join the Jesus restoration movement!

Invite Jesus Christ to possess your body and soul, confessing Him as the Lord *Jesus Christ . . . Solid Rock!*

MEET THE AUTHORS:

- KATHRYN KUHLMAN is seen and heard by millions each week on nationwide TV and radio. Her name is known around the world as the author of two best-selling books, *I Believe in Miracles* and *God Can Do It Again,* both of which witness to supernatural miracles of God today.

  Miss Kuhlman's books have become the most popular reading material in the armed forces, especially in Vietnam. In an age of turmoil and uncertainty, thousands of young people look to her for a word of wisdom. Her strict attention to Bible truth is clearly evident in her contribution to this book.

- HAL LINDSEY is well-known on college campuses as both author and lecturer. His fast selling book, *The Late Great Planet Earth,* has become one of the most widely read books among young Americans today. Few books have done more to focus attention on the credibility of Bible prophecy than this one. His newest book is *Satan Is Alive and Well On Planet Earth,* and it delves even more deeply into the problems of our modern society.

- DAVID WILKERSON is founder of Teen Challenge, an organization started when he began preaching in the streets, in borrowed churches, and in the hideouts of addicts. Today, its headquarters is in a new international complex in Brooklyn. Other centers are strategically located in the United States, Canada, and Europe. He is the author of the best-sellers, *The Cross and the Switchblade*, *Purple Violet Squish*, *Twelve Angels From Hell*, *The Little People*, *Get Your Hands Off My Throat* and *Parents on Trial*.

- W.A. CRISWELL is pastor of one of the largest churches in the world, the influential First Baptist Church of Dallas, Texas. He has studied Bible Prophecy in depth and written widely on the subject. Among his prophetic books are: *Expository Sermons on Daniel* and *Expository Sermons on Revelation*.

- PAT BOONE is one of the most respected entertainers in Hollywood. A very popular figure in leading motion pictures, he recently starred in the hit movie, *The Cross and the Switchblade*. His songs have sold over 30,000,000 albums. Pat Boone is the author of two best-sellers, *'Twix' Twelve and Twenty* and his latest *A New Song*. His Christian testimony is known worldwide.

I BELIEVE IN THE MIRACLE
OF HIS SECOND COMING

1.

I BELIEVE IN THE MIRACLE OF HIS SECOND COMING

KATHRYN KUHLMAN

I want you to realize that the Bible is unlike all other sacred books, because the Bible bases its authority on fulfilled prophecy. Fulfilled prophecy is stronger evidence of the inspiration and the authenticity of the Scriptures than even miracles. And He who has kept His word in the past will keep His promises for the future — believe me — even to the crossing of every *t* and the dotting of every *i*. Therefore, with perfect confidence, we can look forward to that great event that is yet future, *and that is* the Second Coming of the Lord Jesus Christ.

He will return in exactly the same manner as He went away. When He ascended into heaven the first time, He went up bodily and physically in a cloud. He will return to this earth in the clouds.

There are people today who try to explain away this marvelous coming event. They have their own little theories about the coming of the Lord. Such as:

1. "I believe His coming again is spiritual, and that it was fulfilled at the great outpouring of the Holy Spirit on the day of Pentecost." Beloved, it was not Jesus who came at Pentecost — He had just gone away, just a few days prior to that. It was the Holy Spirit who came. Jesus had clearly talked of another personality who was to come at the time of Pentecost: 11

the third person of the Trinity, the Holy Ghost. He is a distinct and separate person from Jesus Christ and from God the Father. That's right! And the fact is, the whole New Testament was written after Pentecost and declares over 160 times that the Second Coming of Christ was still future. So you cannot accept this first theory as truth.

2. There are literally thousands who hold to this next theory: "I believe when a person dies that this is the Second Coming of Christ." But Christ does not come to earth every time there is a death! Why, a soul passes into eternity every second. So this would necessitate Christ's remaining continuously here on earth. The Bible teaches that He is in the position of High Priest at the right hand of God the Father in the heavenlies. The fact is, at death the believer goes to Christ. Christ does not come for the believer. Death is the wages of sin, while the Second Coming of Christ is the manifestation of His *love*. Christ is the Prince of life. There can be no death where He is. Death flees at His coming. His coming is not death, but resurrection! He *is* the resurrection and the life!

3. Then there are those who say, "The Second Coming of Christ takes place in a person's life at the time of his conversion." This cannot be! It couldn't possibly be, for at conversion the sinner comes to Christ — not Christ to the sinner. "Him that cometh unto *Me*," the scripture plainly says. It is true that there *is* such a thing as the spiritual indwelling of Christ in the believer. But His Second Coming, like His first coming, is to be an outward, visible, personal coming. Now that settles that.

So the first question in your mind is WHEN? When is this earth-shaking event going to take place? Well, there are two distinct stages of His Second Coming. The first stage — that great catching up of the believers in the air to meet Christ, which we refer to as the rapture — can take place any day now. It will be a surprise. The average person will not be expecting it. "Watch, therefore, for you know not what hour your Lord doth come."

There have been those people who claim to have a special revelation on the exact day and time of His return. Do not listen to this type of person, for he is in error. There is only One, Jesus said, who knows the exact time: God the Father. And He has not revealed it even to His angels.

However, we do know that so far as unfulfilled prophecy is concerned, the Lord can come any time now without violating any part of the Word of God. No doubt this first stage of Christ's Second Coming will be the next great world event. So we must stay prepared for that great day!

"The Lord Himself shall descend from heaven with a shout, with the voice of the archangel, and with the trump of God: and the dead in Christ shall rise first: Then we which are alive and remain shall be *caught up* together with them *in the clouds,* to meet the Lord *in the air*: and so shall we ever be with the Lord" (I Thessalonians 4:16, 17).

Notice what the scripture says: "in the air, in the clouds." When Christ comes in this first stage, this great catching away, He will not touch the earth. He will come into our atmosphere, and the believers — His followers — will be caught up to meet Him "in the air." The Christians who have been dead for years will be resurrected and join Him in the clouds. And those of us who are alive when He comes will be caught up immediately after the resurrected dead. We will never know death, because we will be translated into immortality by Him. Our bodies will be changed in a moment, in just the twinkling of an eye.

I predict many young people reading this will be immediately turned off. Some of you will call it a fanatic's dream, but your negative reaction doesn't change the truth at all. This world-wide "evacuation" is going to happen whether you believe it or not.

Then comes stage two: the final phase of the Second Coming of Christ. This is the revelation — when Jesus Christ comes back to earth to set up His kingdom. This is how it will happen:

The Lord will return to this earth in bodily form for the first time since He was taken up into heaven, as was described in the last chapter of Luke's gospel. This revelation will be as sudden as was the rapture. The people on earth will not be expecting it.

In the distant heaven there will appear a point of light becoming brighter and brighter as it descends toward the earth. It will appear to be a cloud of dazzling light throwing out flashes of lightning. It will descend on the brow of the Mount of Olives. There the cloud will stop and will unfold before the awe-stricken and terrified beholders. And there will be revealed to the people of the world — Jesus, seated on a white horse. Every eye shall see the Son of Man coming in the clouds of heaven with power and great glory!

You may not want to believe it. Whenever I speak on the Second Coming of Christ, I know there are those people who shrug their shoulders and choose to disbelieve in that which is about to take place. But do you want to know something? You'd better believe it! God's Word says it — and you're a mighty foolish person if you do not accept the Word of God. For the Bible says, "Heaven and earth will pass away, but My Word shall not pass away."

It's going to happen whether you believe it or not. Whether you want it to happen or not. It's going to happen. *It's going to happen!*

A LETTER FROM PAUL
THE APOSTLE:

For with a shout, with the voice of the archangel and the trumpet of God, the Lord Himself will descend from heaven, and those who died in Christ will rise first. Afterward we, the living who remain, will be caught up along with them in the clouds to meet the Lord in the air. And so we shall forever be with the Lord. So then encourage one another with these words.

Concerning times and seasons, brothers, you need no writing from me, for you are yourselves aware that the day of the Lord will come as a thief in the night. When they say, "Peace and safety," then sudden destruction will come upon them like the birthpangs of a pregnant woman, and there will be no escape. You, however, brothers, are not in the dark, so that the day should surprise you like a thief; for you are all sons of light and sons of the day. We belong neither to night nor to darkness. So then, let us not be asleep like the rest, but let us be on our guard and be sober. For those who sleep sleep at night and the drunkards are drunk at night. But as we belong to the day, let us be self-controlled, equipped with faith and love for our breastplate, and the hope of salvation for our helmet. For God has not destined us for His anger, but for the obtaining of salvation through our Lord Jesus Christ, who experienced death for us so that we, whether awake or asleep, might live together with Him. Encourage one another, therefore, and build up one another, as in fact you are doing.

We beg of you, brothers, to recognize the workers among you, those who are leaders in the Lord and your advisers. Because of their work, hold them lovingly in highest regard. Enjoy peace among yourselves. But we appeal to you brothers: warn the idle, encourage the fainthearted, give your support to the weak, exercise patience toward everyone. See to it that no one pays back evil for evil; instead, always try to be helpful to one another and to all people. Always be cheerful. Pray unceasingly. Under all circumstances give thanks, for such is God's will for you in Christ Jesus. Do not stifle the Spirit. Do not despise prophetic utterance, but test it all and retain what is good. Keep away from evil in every form.

And may the God of peace Himself make you holy through and through. May your whole being — spirit, soul, and body — be kept blameless at the coming of our Lord Jesus Christ. He who calls you is faithful and He will accomplish it.

Brothers, pray for us. Greet all the brothers with a sacred kiss. I solemnly charge you in the Lord's name to have this letter read to all the brothers.

The grace of our Lord Jesus Christ be with you.

Sincerely,

Paul the Apostle

(I Thessalonians 4:16-18; 5:1-28 —
The Modern Language Bible)

EXTINCTION
OR EVACUATION

2.

EXTINCTION OR EVACUATION

HAL LINDSEY

We have just entered the most electrifying decade of human history. The 1970's are the most determinative decade of history — for the die is being cast as to how it will end.

We have enough evidence available today to show us that man is headed toward some sort of catastrophic climax in his long history. Knowledgable people are saying that man will probably not survive this century. Population explosion, pollution, ecological imbalance, nuclear threat all point to the end of time.

There is a time limit on the human race from the standpoint of pollution and from the standpoint of population. And there is another great problem we are up against — the nuclear threat.

Whenever scientists and statesmen speak of the dangers confronting *this generation*, they all point to the fact that we will reach a critical point by the mid-70's and a catastrophic point by the turn of the century.

If we are headed toward an obvious climax in history, there must be something in the Bible about it. There are events today which, because they are happening all at once, are different from any other time in history. We are seeing the final fitting together of all the prophetic signs that Jesus said would come.

THE FIRST SIGN: ISRAEL To BECOME a NATION

This one is the most important. If this sign were not present in the world today, nothing else would be relevant. Every generation has had some of the signs of the return of the Messiah — so that it has always seemed that He might come in their time. But there never has been a time before this generation when this first sign has appeared. It is the warning of God's timepiece, Israel. Moses first predicted that because the people of Israel would not believe God and would turn away from Him, they would be scattered around the world. He said a great nation would come and take them captive and they would serve this nation, while their own nation would be destroyed. This is the first part of a two-part prophecy regarding Israel's history.

Other prophets added details. The dispersion of the people occurred in 600 B.C. when the Babylonian Nebuchadnezzar swept in and took the Jewish people captive. Jerusalem, along with the temple, was utterly destroyed. In Babylon the Jews were held against their will for exactly seventy years, just as Jeremiah the prophet had predicted (Jeremiah 25:8-10).

Just as Moses predicted (and Jesus added more detail), Titus and the Roman legion totally crushed the Jewish people in A.D. 70. The Romans destroyed Jerusalem and sold the survivors into slavery, dispersing them throughout the world and into exile that has lasted to this present hour.

In Ezekiel 36, the prophet predicts that just shortly before the Messiah will return and set up God's kingdom here on earth, these scattered Jewish people will return to become a nation again (Ezekiel 36:16-18).

Jesus the Messiah (before He was taken to be crucified), in speaking of the events that would immediately precede His return, told of the return of the Jews to the land of Palestine. As a nation, He said, they would be in possession of old Jerusalem. Now remember that! He also said that this generation which saw the Jews back in their land and in possession of old Jerusalem *would see His return!* That is what Ezekiel was predicting 2600 years ago.

When the Jews became a nation again in 1948, that was the most important sign any generation could see.

THE SECOND SIGN: JEWS RETURN to OLD JERUSALEM

The second sign is this: before the Messiah can return, the Jews have to possess old Jerusalem, for much of the warfare in the last war of the world will be *over the city of Jerusalem.* Zechariah (12-14) writes about the battle of Jerusalem, one of the campaigns of Armageddon, the War of Wars! He tells us in Chapter 12:2-4 that this last war of the world is triggered over a dispute about who owns Jerusalem. Now mind you, Zechariah was writing 500 years before Jesus was born.

The whole purpose of the Six Day War was to get old Jerusalem back again. Do you realize that for the first time in 2500 years the Jews have total possession and sovereign control of old Jerusalem? They have never totally controlled it since they were taken to Babylon by Nebuchadnezzar. And yet they have it *now.*

Since these first two signs have set the stage for the coming again of Jesus the Messiah, every other sign I am going to give you has great significance. If the first two things were not true, the other signs would have no more significance than they had in 1940 or any other time. But you see, there has never been a time before when the Jew has been returned from a world-wide dispersion and been in total possession of old Jerusalem.

THE THIRD SIGN: REBUILDING of the TEMPLE

The third sign has not yet happened, but it will soon. The Jew is to rebuild the temple again in old Jerusalem. He has to. In 2 Thessalonians 2, Paul speaks of the great world dictator, that future Fuehrer who is to come. Paul speaks of this man taking a seat in the temple of God and declaring himself to be God. The temple of God can only be the temple in old Jerusalem. Jesus speaks of the environs of the temple in Matthew 24:15-16. He speaks of the "abomination of desolation" which Daniel the prophet predicted. This "abomination of desolation" is a Jewish technical term meaning the desecration of the temple's holy place. For the Antichrist to desecrate the temple, there first has to be a temple. Documents discovered last year, after the repossession of the temple area, gave the exact methodology of cutting the stones for the temple. They had been buried for centuries near the Wailing Wall. Now the temple can be prefabricated in about six months.

THE FOURTH SIGN: A RUSSIAN ATTACK on ISRAEL

The fourth sign could only happen after the Jews were a nation again in their ancient homeland. Ezekiel (Chapter 38) predicts the restoring of the people as a nation. He said that after the Jews are returned from this dispersion, there is going to arise a fantastic power from their uttermost north. This northern nation would become their arch-enemy and this nation would actually be involved in a direct attack upon Israel, triggering the last war of the world.

Men who have studied this passage have identified this power by ethnic background. Meshech, Magog, and Tubal are tribal names as old as history itself. These tribes are descendants of Japheth, the son of Noah, and are named in Genesis 10. William Gesenius, expert on ancient Hebrew, declares, "This is referring to the tribes that now form the Russian people."

Russia is the only nation to the uttermost north of Israel. If you take a globe and go directly north, you will end right in the middle of Russia. If you want to read the future of Russia, I can tell you exactly what is going to happen to Russia and its Communist confederacies. All of Russia's confederates are mentioned, including the Arabs.

THE FIFTH SIGN: A FINAL ARAB-ISRAELI WAR

The fifth sign is this: at the same time this northern power will arise, there will develop a confederacy of Arabs who will unite in common hatred of the nation. Finally, they will actually launch the attack against the nation of Israel, bringing about the last war of the world.

The time of the end is defined for us in Daniel. It is the time when Christ comes back. The king of the south is also identified for us in this chapter. He is Egypt in league with the Arab nations —and Egypt will be the leader. The king of the north (Russia) will stretch out his hands against the countries, and the land of Egypt will not escape. Russia is going to double-cross the Egyptians. Russia will become ruler of the wealth-filled treasuries of Egypt. The Libyans and the Ethiopians will also be captured. The words in the Hebrew translated as "Libyan" and "Ethiopian" do not mean what we think of today as the countries of Libya and Ethiopia. These words refer to a whole race of people. The word translated as "Libyan" means the African Arabs — all of them. The word in the Hebrew translated as "Ethiopian" is the word "Cush," which means "black man," and is talking about the Black Africans.

Russia, with its confederates, is going to make a lightning-like thrust through the Middle East and conquer the whole African continent. Then Daniel said, "But (while Russia is doing all of this conquest of the African continent) reports from the East and from the North shall alarm him so that he (the Russian) shall withdraw in great fury to destroy and annihilate many." (MLB) While the Russian army is down in Egypt and Africa, news from the north and east will trouble it. If you look to the north of Africa, what do you see? Europe. And as you look to the east, you see Asia.

THE SIXTH SIGN: CHINA WILL ENTER the MID-EAST WAR

While all of this is going on, there will be a great confederacy of Asians formed. They are going to come into this battle once the Arabs and the Russians begin. Revelation 16:12-14 tells us about their entrance on the scene. The kings of the east will come and stage their armies on the banks of the Euphrates River.

That is the news which comes from the east to trouble the Russians. Revelation 9 tells us in symbolic language that a vast army will come from the Euphrates River. This eastern power will build an army of 200,000,000 soldiers. *China, right now, boasts a militia of 200,000,000 soldiers!* India is taking Pakistan to the UN General Assembly because Pakistan was cooperating with the Red Chinese to build a road over the mountains which separate them, a road connecting the Red Chinese with the subcontinent — a straight shot to the Euphrates River.

THE SEVENTH SIGN: A NEW EUROPEAN CONFEDERACY and WORLD DICTATOR

The Bible predicts that ancient Rome will be revived again just shortly before the coming of Christ. Daniel 7:15-25 gives a description of this. In the last days ten nations will rise up out of ruins of the old Roman empire. These ten nations, descendants of the old Roman empire, will join together in a confederacy.

They will become a vast economic and industrial power. But the real power will come when out of these ten nations, or this Roman culture, will suddenly arise an electrifying leader: I call him the future Fuehrer; some call him the Antichrist. There is a great deal given in the Scriptures about this person, the Antichrist. Scripture says that the ten-nation confederacy, which is basically Western Europe, will come up first. Then this dictator will take it over and weld it into a world-conquering power.

I believe that the European Common Market is the foundation for the revival of Rome and the ten-nation confederacy. Just recently it was announced that by the mid-70's the Common Market expects to add four more nations. That will make ten! A French foreign minister recently said: "The Europe of the future, when it finally unites politically as well as economically, will be the mightiest force on earth."

Somewhere in Europe, right now, lives the greatest leader this world will ever know — outside of Jesus the Messiah. Somewhere in Europe there is a man who will make Hitler look like a *choir boy!* But this man, according to the profile the Scripture gives him, is going to appear to be the savior of the world. People are going to accept him as a deity. He is going to come with an electrifying program. We are even told what the main thrust of his promises will be.

The first promise will be *to free the world of war.* He will bring universal peace. The second promise has to do with providing *an answer to the economic problems* that will plague the earth, and that will include the problem of food. He will have genuine answers — but worship of himself will be the price tag. He will force every person in the world to swear allegiance to him as god, or they cannot receive a number. And if they don't get that number, they can't buy or sell or hold a job.

The greatest and most fantastic event ever to occur on this earth will take place just shortly before the Roman dictator is revealed. In I Corinthians 15:51 the apostle Paul said, "Behold, I show you a mystery." In other words, I am going to show you something that has never been revealed before and that only a Christian can understand. He said, "We shall not all sleep (die), but we shall all be changed." The Lord will give a shout, and we will be caught up in the air and will be changed from mortal to immortal. Suddenly we will be face to face with the Lord!

The Bible speaks of the fact that the institutional church will get worse and worse just shortly before Christ takes the real Christians out of the world. All the churches will then be brought into the one-world religion. This will be the foundation of a great religion which will be the revival of MYSTERY BABYLON (a religion founded on astrology, witchcraft, and later, drug addiction). The root of this evil religion (as Revelation describes it) is already imbedded in our present culture.

The part that is very important to note is the Bible says there will be a tremendous number of people who, when they become afraid of all the things they see, are going to respond to the claims of Christ. Just before the taking up of the true Christians there is going to be perhaps the greatest time of evangelism ever known here on earth.

These new Christians are not going to change the world, because the world is going to hate them and put them to death. We are approaching a time when you are going to be killed for being a Christian. It is already happening in much of the world today.

No matter the cost, it will be worth it all: to leave this messed-up world and join Christ in looking after the needs of His limitless universe.

*Adapted from the Late Great Planet Earth ©1970 by Zondervan Publishing House, and Homo Sapiens, Extinction or Evacuation, ©1970, 1971, Christian Information Committee, Berkeley, Cal., also published by Zondervan. Used by permission.

CHILDREN
OF THE BOMB

3.

CHILDREN
OF THE BOMB

DAVID WILKERSON

"We are in the first phase of what is perhaps the pen-
ultimate revolution. Its next phase may be atomic warfare." — Aldous Huxley

There is no predictable future for them. They are
living under the burden of change. There is confusion
everywhere, verging on total chaos: no center to
things — no shared belief.

To call it a revolution is too simple: Something is
happening deeper than that. It touches every aspect
of life: Sex, religion, politics and all the senses. It is
multi-dimensional and mysterious. In some way it has
to do with rediscovering *oneself,* along with a foyer
into the mystery of the cosmos.

These youth are a class — a tribal class: Thinking
of themselves as exploited, abused, processed.

"Things are in the saddle and they ride mankind."
— Emerson

Believing elders have failed them, they learn from
one another. They despise the old traditional ways of
life claiming they led to cesspools in Vietnam and
Chicago. Stubbornly determined not to be ruled by
anyone, they repudiate most of the basic assump-
tions of society. Down on all systems that stimulate

greed, sex desires that cannot be satisfied, hatred with no outlet but in violence, they feel like prisoners on this earth: Worrying about their impotence to change things with no one to comfort them about tomorrow.

"We see all around us a terrible alienation of the best and bravest of our young; the very shape of a generation seems turned on its head overnight." — The late Robert Kennedy

Phony religion only intensifies their confusion; easy and early sexuality swallowed them up; they were trapped in a web of new ideas; drugs became a way out of the jungle — an escape from institutions geared to another generation.

They were unable to change the establishment through rage, so they tried to melt into a landscape of fantasy; through psychedelic adventures find a new revelation. They were hoping to discard their old identity and take on another. Thus, a strange kind of brotherhood developed with promise of dramatic and enchanting forms of reality. Drug abuse became a shared experience — a group ride into risky currents.

"PRESIDENT SAYS DRUGS NO. 1 PROBLEM"

But the feeling of freedom was empty when all believable authority dissolved and everything was replaced by experimental experience. This false freedom was unmasked and exposed. They had become gods to themselves. Free souls took to the mountains and deserts. They ran from God, from homes and parents, simply hitchhiking or riding freight trains . . . away . . . just to see what lies beyond the next hill. All the guides to life were lost or abandoned. That is how it happened.

Beginning in the early sixties we began to reap the failure of the fifties. The children of the bomb suddenly split — acidheads and potheads replaced eggheads. Junkies and rebels became heroes. It became a "high" society whose members turned from Billy Graham to Timothy Leary.

Dropping out became a religious experience — hard kicks replaced soft kicks: Young people flirted with the outer perimeter of existence.

Flights from reality chipped away at their hearts, emptying them of hope and belief; life became nothing but an empty outline. Eaten with an inner intensity they could not name, children of the bomb lived with absolute annihilation spreading that indelible stain on everything they touched. World crises and assassinations and civil wars all brought new feelings of alienation and hopelessness.

"Are we witnessing the final act of a Greek tragedy, with the chorus warning of the impending disaster, but helpless to act? Maybe we are." — Erich Fromm

The hypocrisy of high dignitaries and the immorality of the new world church cut them off from the root source of life. The children of the bomb have been radicalized. Introduced by the underground to one view of issues. Tossing insults at non-liberated people, they have become polarized and crystallized; A nation within a nation, clustered in big city Bohemias, "Love is alive and hiding in San Francisco."

Fighting off malnutrition and VD, migrating across continents, fleeing from an unnamed enemy, seeking an undefined haven, running from the bosom of middle class obesity, tired of superficial fashion hangups promoted by dollar-mad manufacturers, they parade in curious costumes and wild dress, blasting intellectuals, liberals, and the establishment alike. 31

Unwilling to punch a clock for industry (while their fathers sever the tie between work and wages), their nervous systems have been shattered by news media panic and rumors of war. So they have turned to a romantic infatuation with guerrilla warfare: a misty-eyed involvement in power struggles, enchantment with the teaching of Mao and Che Gueverra.

"CRIES OF 'CHE' TAUNT VICE PRESIDENT"

They feel the empire is crumbling as did all others in history. So the continents are up for grabs. They believe the country is coming down and will die off like an insect. So they want to go down making love, and singing in the face of the apocalypse. You see this new breed sitting in hordes all over the world waiting for a suicidal, killer world to end.

"Blood and fire, and pillars of smoke." — Joel the Prophet

Not a word has to be spoken between them. It is an inner message they have all received: *The end is near,* and organized religion doesn't have a ghost of a chance to reach them in their bankruptcy.

All hope is gone — every door shut. Except One!

JESUS CHRIST — THE SOLID ROCK

He is now restoring — uniting — healing. His presence is now an international issue. Thousands of revolutionaries have been captured by Him! Christ is whacking the powers that be! Change is in the air!

False clergymen are sweating in their starchy collars, while a Jesus phenomenon punctures their dogma. Mao's Red bible is being exchanged for God's Holy Bible. There is even a stirring in the dirt: Junkies, harlots, hippies, and freaks now preach, praise, and pray.

has replaced Jesus Christ Superstar. Heaven's Western Union has telegraphed a message, and the children of the bomb are receiving it loud and clear: Jesus Christ will soon return to enlist an army of believers, raptured in the twinkling of an eye to meet Him mid-air in the cosmos. And it shall be even as the Scriptures promise:

Whosoever will call upon the name of the Lord
Shall be saved.

"This really revolutionary revolution is to be achieved, not in the external world, but in the souls and flesh of human beings." — Aldous Huxley

THE WORLD'S
GREATEST MYSTERY

4.

THE WORLD'S GREATEST MYSTERY

DAVID WILKERSON

The world's greatest mystery is about to be solved. It will involve a miracle so big, so vast, so out of sight — only real Jesus people can believe it!

And this is it: God is going to change millions of human bodies from every nation into celestial bodies in a split second's time!

> Behold, I show you a mystery; we shall not all sleep, but we shall all be changed . . . in a moment, in the twinkling of an eye, at the last trump: for the trumpet shall sound, and the dead shall be raised incorruptible, and we shall be changed.
> (1 Corinthians 15:51-2).

It staggers the human mind! But believe it or not — here is exactly what the Bible says is going to happen:

1. Corrupted, diseased, cancerous bodies will be suddenly transformed into incorruptible, perfect, celestial bodies.

2. Cripples will get new, perfect limbs. Old, decrepit bodies will be instantly made into perfect, holy bodies.

3. The grave of every true Christian will break open. In a split second, all the dead believers from every tribe and nation will be raised with new bodies.

4. Immediately after the dead are raised, we who are alive and believe will suddenly vanish from the earth, encased in a new body. We will be caught up to meet Christ in the air.

UNBELIEVABLE? A fantastic fairy tale? A put-on mystery concocted by a fanatic? A cruel hoax?

NOT ON YOUR LIFE! Read it again: it's all in your Bible:

> "We shall all be changed — in a moment — in the twinkling of an eye . . ."

This mysterious and miraculous change will take place in three distinct happenings. Two of these are *already being experienced* — and the last can happen at any time now!

Any living person on earth can get in on this miracle during the first two happenings, but only committed Jesus people can participate in the third stage. These three happenings are clearly predicted in every Bible:

Happening Number One:
A JESUS RESTORATION MOVEMENT!

The Jesus movements now sweeping the earth have been started by the Holy Spirit *to prepare the nations for the return of Jesus Christ.* The ancient prophet Joel predicted that immediately prior to the coming of Christ an army of Jesus people would be raised up to prepare the way. They would be commissioned to make a midnight cry to "go out and meet Him." Here is how the prophet of God described this army of Jesus people.

Joel, Chapter Two

They will sound an alarm that judgment is near.

It will be a great and powerful army — the likes of them have not been seen before,

And never will throughout the generations of the world!

They will upset the calm and peace of the land:
Like warriors mounted on horses they will march
　　Almost like a fire raging across the fields!
The world will be afraid of them
　　Because they charge like infantry men.
They climb over every obstacle like commandoes.
　　Refusing to break rank — never crowding one
another,
　　Each person is right in his place.
No leader but one chief commander,
　　God!
They swarm over cities, mountains, walls,
　　Everywhere they go they shake things up!
They will shine so brightly it will obscure the sun
and stars.
　　The Lord will lead them with a shout.
It is His army, and they obey His orders —
　　They know the day of the Lord is at hand!
And no one can endure that awesome day,
　　So they all preach one message:

"Turn to the Lord Jesus Christ while there is still time.
Give Him all your heart. Come and surrender to Him.
Repent and change your life. The Lord is merciful and
kind — full of forgiveness and love. He does not want
to punish or hurt you — so He calls you in love. Whosoever shall call upon His name shall be saved from
judgment."

Thousands of young people around the world have
joined the Jesus army. Drug abusers quit using nar-
cotics. Pot heads and acid freaks began to study their
Bibles and surrendered to Christ. Runaways and
hippies turned to the Lord and found what they were
looking for. Campus atheists and SDS members
opened their minds and hearts and invited Jesus
Christ in. Now, students everywhere are a part of
this army of Jesus people.
　　Why did it happen so suddenly? Why is it spreading
to every nation? What does it all mean?

- It means the Holy Spirit has set up office to enlist an army of former sinners (He has restored those who heeded the call to enlist) and they have been chosen to warn the world that time is up!

- This restoration army is not made up of crazy fanatics. They do not preach a doomsday message of fear. All they are saying is this: "It's the midnight hour for this old earth. Judgment is coming — but Christ wants to save you. Give up, while there is time."

Happening Number Two:
THE HOLY SPIRIT OUTPOURING UPON ALL FLESH!

There is going to be a deluge of the Holy Spirit upon every man, woman, boy, and girl on the face of this earth.

> "In the last days, God said, I will pour out of my Holy Spirit upon *all* mankind . . ." (Acts 2:17).

When this happens, we are to know then that the return of Jesus Christ is right at the door. He is coming right after the Holy Spirit is poured out. And when the Holy Spirit is poured out three things will happen:

1. He will convince every human being of his sin;
2. He will reveal the availability of God's goodness and grace;
3. He will convince men that they can be delivered from the certain coming judgment.

   "And when he is come (the Holy Spirit), He will convince the world of its sin, and of the availability of God's goodness, and of deliverance from judgment . . ."

(John 16:8)

According to God's Word, it appears that a certain limited time has been set (perhaps just a few weeks or months) in which it is possible every human being

40

will experience an "overwhelming" by the Holy Spirit:

- Every Moslem and Jew;
- Politicians, world leaders, and dictators;
- Rich and poor — black, white, red, yellow;
- Every criminal behind bars, every prostitute on the street;
- Students, professors, ministers, labor leaders;
- The old and feeble, the young and strong;
- Russians, Chinese, Africans, Indians and Europeans: Every breathing soul should experience this unusual happening.
- It is probable that every person on earth will be convinced by the Holy Spirit of his sins.
- Everywhere the gospel message has been heard the Spirit of God will convict men of its truth.
- There will be a silent, world-wide call to repent and prepare.
- Men will instinctively know they can be spared judgment if they only look up to Him for deliverance.
- (The concept of instinctive knowledge of God was first explained by the Apostle Paul in Romans.) "But God shows his anger from heaven against all sinful, evil men who push away the truth from them. For the truth about God is known to them instinctively; God has put this knowledge in their hearts".

(Romans 1:18-19 Amp.).

"For this reason you are without excuse, O man, every one who judges, for you condemn yourself in that in which you judge the other, for you who judge do the same things"

(Romans 2:1).

- Every person must either respond or reject the Spirit's call. The rejectors will shake off the conviction by saying:

"But where is the sign of His coming — for things continue as they were from the beginning of time?"

The rejectors will be turned over to a hard heart and a reprobate mind. Their chances will be lost forever, sealing their own doom. They will become pleasure mad and sensuous and will laugh at the very thought of judgment and death. They will turn to an antichrist and fill the earth with sex, perversion, crime and violence.

But those who respond will become new people. They will be changed now to prepare for the great change that is soon to come. Many are called into the restoration movement — but only a few of these called ones will obey the Spirit in the end and enter the straight and narrow gate. It is possible to be restored from an old sinful life, delivered from evil habits, join the Jesus people, but still be lost when Christ returns. Listen! When the Holy Spirit comes upon you, He says:

"Come out from among them and be ye separate and clean — then I will receive you."

Clean up your hands and purify your heart! Then you need never fear God's judgment!

Happening Number Three:
THE RETURN OF JESUS CHRIST TO CAPTURE THE CHRISTIANS!

The world's greatest mystery will end in the twinkling of an eye. The trumpet of God will sound, and Christ will appear in the heavens to rapture His children from the earth. The Holy Spirit will end His work, ceasing to strive with and convict men. We who trust and believe will vanish in a fraction of a second and be changed. We will leave the earth and meet our Lord and Savior in the atmosphere.

When this will happen exactly has not been revealed to men. But God did give certain clues (or signs) that would pinpoint the approximate time of Christ's return. In fact, Christians have been commanded to "Look up and rejoice when these signs begin to happen, because redemption and rapture is near." Not only have all these signs of His return begun — they have nearly been fulfilled. This can only mean the earth is living on borrowed time. The clock has already touched midnight.

• God gave us the "**Prosperity sign**":

"As it was in the days of Noah, so shall it also be in the day when Christ shall come."

How was it then?

They were drunkards and gluttons.

They were playing games of marriage and divorce. It was a time of great prosperity and a construction boom. They were absorbed in trade, merchandise, and fashion. If Noah lived today, he would cry:

"It is just as in my day — The hour has come — Seal your ark and prepare to leave."

• The "**Peace sign**":

"When men shall cry peace — peace and safety — then shall the end come . . ."

A peace movement will arise in the last day.

Men will be crying and sighing to live in safety

From bombs, threats, wars, and rumors of wars.

Look all around you today.

See the thousands who have joined the peace movements,

And remember, God said:

"Peace shall become a by-word, a sign of greeting: This means Christ's coming is near."

● The "Violence sign": (II Peter 2)

We are warned to beware of a time when men will:
Despise government,
  riot in the daytime,
speak evil of those in authority,
  speak swelling words of vanity,
seduce the innocent and mock righteousness,
  laugh at and flirt with evil powers,
live in sin while sitting in on the Jesus festivals,
  proudly boast of their perversion and sin.

Now any intelligent person knows these very things are all reflected in today's newspaper. These signs are happening all around us and should be our final warning of His return.

The clues are all in. The last call has gone out. Now it's all up to you. The only important question left is this:

"Will you be ready to go when He comes?"

You must answer that question today! You can't put it off any longer.

BEWARE OF
PHONY JESUS PEOPLE

BEWARE OF
PHONY JESUS PEOPLE

The Bible predicts: Satan will attempt to infiltrate the Jesus restoration movement with *phonies*.

Now Hear This:

Not everyone who uses My name will enter the Kingdom of heaven — but he that doeth the will of My Father. Yet many will come on that final day saying, "Lord, we preached in your name!" "We did miracles in Jesus's name!" "We cast out devils!" "We did many wonderful works!" But the Lord will say to them, "Depart from me, you indulgers in sin. I never even knew you."

Woe unto you, hypocrites and Pharisees! You pretend to be holy with your long public demonstrations and prayers. You try to look saintly and pious, but under your robes you are besmirched with every sort of hypocrisy and sin. You go to all lengths to make one convert, then turn him into twice the son of hell you are. You tithe and keep the law to the last letter, but you forget the more important things: Justice, Mercy, and Faith. You strain at gnats and swallow camels. You polish the outside, but the inside is foul and corrupt.

False prophets shall arise and lead many astray, doing wonderful miracles — attempting to deceive even God's elect. I have warned you: by their fruits you shall know them — where there is confusion and division there is evil work. You would think these phonies were Moses the way they keep making up so many laws and making people obey their every whim. DON'T follow their example! They load you with impossible demands, and don't try to keep them themselves. All they do is for show.

The true test is LOVE. For if any man love not his brother, the love of God is not in him. He is a phony! (From Matthew 23 and 24 — adapted from *The Modern Language Bible*)

THE BATTLE OF
ARMAGEDDON

THE BATTLE OF ARMAGEDDON

W. A. CRISWELL

11 And I saw heaven opened, and behold a white horse; and he that sat upon him was called Faithful and True; and in righteousness he doth judge and make war.

12 His eyes were as a flame of fire, and on his head were many crowns; and he had a name written, that no man knew, but he himself.

13 And he was clothed with a vesture dipped in blood: and his name is called The Word of God.

14 And the armies which were in heaven followed him upon white horses, clothed in fine linen, white and clean.

15 And out of his mouth goeth a sharp sword, that with it he should smite the nations: and he shall rule them with a rod of iron: and he treadeth the winepress of the fierceness and wrath of Almighty God.

16 And he hath on his vesture and on his thigh a name written, KING OF KINGS, AND LORD OF LORDS.

17 And I saw an angel standing in the sun; and he cried with a loud voice, saying to all the fowls that fly in the midst of heaven, Come and gather yourselves together unto the supper of the great God;

18 That ye may eat the flesh of kings, and the flesh of captains, and the flesh of mighty men, and the flesh of horses, and of them that sit on them, and the flesh of all men, both free and bond, both small and great.

19 And I saw the beast, and the kings of the earth, and their armies, gathered together to make war against him that sat on the horse, and against his army.

20 And the beast was taken, and with him the false prophet that wrought miracles before him, with which he deceived them that had received the mark of the beast, and them that worshipped his image. These both were cast alive into a lake of fire burning with brimstone.

21 And the remnant were slain with the sword of him that sat upon the horse, which sword proceeded out of his mouth: and all the fowls were filled with their flesh. (Revelation 19:11-21)

What an unimaginable catastrophe! What death and carnage! This vast holocaust closes human history.

The Battle of Armageddon, the War of Megiddo, is the scene in which the great God and Savior Jesus Christ appears, intervening in human history. The first verses of chapter 19 of the Revelation recount the marriage supper of the Lamb, which supper is preceded by the marriage of the Son of God to His bride, who has made herself ready. Speedily and immediately after the marriage of the Lamb and after the nuptial supper, the gates of heaven burst open in the triumph of the hosts of glory. As Jude said in verses 14 and 15, "Behold, the Lord cometh with ten thousands of his saints, To execute judgment upon all." Immediately after the wedding supper, our Lord appears in glory with His angelic hosts and with His saints. He intervenes in this awesome, catastrophic holocaust that God calls the Battle of Armageddon. Notice that history does not quietly and gradually merge into the kingdom of our Messiah. The end comes violently; it comes in fury. The whole earth is bathed in blood, in the judgment of the great day of God Almighty.

THE FINAL BATTLE DESCRIBED THROUGHOUT THE BIBLE

The mighty conflict described here in chapter 19 of the Revelation is one that has been foretold all through the Bible. The book of the Revelation is the unveiling, the presentation of Jesus Christ at the consummation of the age. And prophecy, in the Old Testament and in the New Testament, without exception, says that the end of this world comes in a vast, mighty, indescribable conflict. World history ends in war and desolation.

This great battle called Armageddon has been described several times previously in the book of the Revelation. For example, in Revelation 11:15 we read, at the sounding of the seventh trumpet: "And the seventh angel sounded; and there were great voices in heaven, saying, The kingdoms of this world are become the kingdoms of our Lord, and of his Christ; and he shall reign for ever and ever." Then follows a description of His reign: "And the four and twenty elders, which sat before God on their seats, fell upon their faces, and worshipped God, Saying, We give thee thanks, O Lord God Almighty . . . because thou hast taken to thee thy great power, and hast reigned. And the nations were angry . . . (because the time has come when God) shouldest destroy them which destroy the earth." These last words refer to that great and final battle. The conflict is mentioned again in Revelation 14:17-20: "And another angel came out of the temple . . . And another angel came out from the altar, which had power over fire; and cried with a loud cry to him that had the sharp sickle, saying, Thrust in thy sharp sickle, and gather the clusters of the vine of the earth· for her grapes are fully ripe. And the angel thrust in his sickle into the earth, and gathered the vine of the earth, and cast it into the great winepress of the wrath of God. And the winepress was trodden without the city, and blood came out." (Notice that grapes cast into a winepress is the figure, but when the grapes are trodden in the wrath and judgment of God, blood pours out.) "And the winepress was trodden . . . and blood came out of the winepress, even unto the horse bridles, by the space of a thousand and six furlongs." A furlong is an eighth of a mile. Divide eight into sixteen hundred and the result is two hundred miles. Blood up to the bridles of the horses for two hundred miles! It is unimaginable. The world has never read of it, has never conceived, it has never seen anything comparable to this last, great battle that will destroy apostate humanity.

There is another reference to this last conflict in Revelation 16:12-16. "And the sixth angel poured out his vial upon the great river Euphrates; and the water thereof was dried up, that the way of the kings of the east might be prepared." They are coming from the north, the south, the east, and the west by the millions. "And I saw three unclean spirits like frogs come out of the mouth of the dragon, and out of the mouth of the beast, and out of the mouth of the false prophet. For they are the spirits of devils, working miracles, which go forth unto the kings of the earth and of the whole world, to gather them to the battle of that great day of God Almighty . . . And he gathered them together into a place called in the Hebrew tongue Armageddon." Revelation 9:16 describes the army of one of the kings: "And the number of the army of the horsemen were two hundred thousand thousand: and I heard the number of them." Two hundred million. It is unbelievable, it is unimaginable. "He gathered them together in a place called in the Hebrew tongue *har megiddo* — 'the mountain of Megiddo,'" which is before the valley of Esdraelon.

These passages in the Revelation add vivid details to the account of the battle described in the text here in Chapter 19.

This Battle of Armageddon, the final conflict that dissolves human history and at which time Christ comes from heaven in glory and in great power, is referred to time and again in Old Testament prophecies. For example, Isaiah 63:1: "Who is this that cometh from Edom, with dyed garments from Bozrah? this that is glorious in his apparel, travelling in the greatness of his strength?" Then Isaiah, looking at him, notices that he is stained with blood. "Wherefore art thou red in thine apparel, and thy garments like him that treadeth in the winefat?" Dyed red. The Almighty Warrior replies: "I have trodden the winepress alone . . . and their blood shall be sprinkled upon my garments, and I will stain all my raiment . . . And I will tread down the people in mine anger, and make them drunk in my fury, and I will bring down their strength to the earth." Crush it into the dust of the ground. This is the battle of the great day of God Almighty.

In Ezekiel 38 and 39 we read of that same vast destruction. In Daniel 2, 7, 9 and 11 are references to the same great holocaust. We meet it again in the third chapter of the book of Joel: "Proclaim ye this among the Gentiles; Prepare war, wake up the mighty men, let all the men of war draw near; let them come up: Beat your plowshares into swords, and your pruninghooks into spears; let the weak say, I am strong. Assemble yourselves . . . . Let the heathen be wakened, and come up to the valley of Jehoshaphat . . . . The sun and moon shall be darkened, and the stars shall withdraw their shining . . . and the heavens and the earth shall shake: but the Lord will be the hope of his people." Then, of course, in Zecha-

55

riah 14:1, 2, 4, 5: "Behold, the day of the Lord cometh
. . . . For I will gather all nations against Jerusalem to
battle . . . . And his feet shall stand in that day upon
the mount of Olives . . . . and the Lord my God shall
come, and all the saints with thee."

The prophets with one accord say that the armies
of the earth will be assembled in Palestine. They will
gather from one end of the globe to the other. The
king of the north is coming down; that is Russia. The
king of the west is coming over; that is the leadership
of the nations of the confederated European states of
which we are a part. The United States belongs to
the federation of the west. We shall always be identified with Europe, always. We belong to it. And the
kings of the east shall come. One of those armies
(Revelation 9:16) numbers two hundred million. The
king of the south is coming; that is Africa and all of
the nations of that vast continent. These armies will
be converging on Palestine. Enemies will gather from
every side. It will be a war to exterminate Israel; it
will be a war of nation against nation; and it will be
a war against God.

The great rendezvous, the great assembly of those
hosts will be at Megiddo. That is the battlefield of the
world, Megiddo. There Barak and Deborah fought
against Sisera. There Gideon fought against the Mid-
ianites. There Saul was slain at the hand of the
Philistines. There Ahaziah was slain by the arrows of
Jehu. There Pharaoh Necho slew good King Josiah.
There Jeremiah lamented the slain of the armies of
Josiah. And through the ages since, each battle fought
there, whether by the Druses or the Turks or the
armies of Napoleon, is a harbinger of the great day
of the battle of God Almighty.

In the King James Version, the Greek word *polemos*
in Revelation 16:14 is translated "battle." We are

apt to think of that translation in terms of one isolated skirmish. The word, rather, is actually "war." The whole earth is plunged into a vast militarism. There is the spirit and the march of slaughter, murder, bloodshed and violence among all mankind. This is the *polemos,* the war of the great day of God Almighty. It has many phases and many parts and the whole earth is involved in it. That is why a man who reads the Bible and looks out over the world today and sees the immeasurable preparation for war is not taken by surprise. It is the development of history according to the prophets. And America is in it to the hilt. Why do you think we have already spent billions of dollars to get a man to the moon? Just for the sake of a joy ride up there? No! We are spending billions of dollars to place men on the moon simply because, if we do not, we lie a prey to those who are able to explore space and thereby able to send enemy craft over our nation to pinpoint a bomb on any city or installation in our land. It is a matter of self-defense; it is a matter of survival. This whole earth is getting ready for war. That is why we are forced to spend money on space exploration. That is why France is trying to build an independent nuclear deterrent. It is national defense.

Always remember, there is no such thing as having instruments of war and not using them. Whenever you build a tank, you are going to use it some day. Whenever you invent a gun, you are going to shoot it some day. When the scientists were trying to split the atom and thus discover nuclear power, the prophecy was made that if it was ever achieved it would first be used in an atomic bomb. Was atomic fission first used to manufacture electricity? Was atomic power first used for peaceful purposes? No. It was used in war. Thus, the whole earth is getting 57 ready for a final holocaust. When we read the Word of the Lord, then look at the newspapers, we tremble in the presence of the prophets who describe this terrible coming day.

THE VICTORIOUS WARRIOR CHRIST

Now, let us look at the text more closely. First, in the midst of that terrible and indescribable conflict, there is the bursting open of heaven and the appearing of the Son of God. He is thus described: "His eyes were like a flame of fire [burning fire, probing into the darkest recesses of the human soul], and on his head were many crowns." One could preach a sermon on the diadems that rest so marvelously and appropriately upon the brow of the Son of God.

Next we read, ". . . and he had a name written, that no man knew, but he himself." That refers to His essential deity, the uncommunicable, unpronouncable, unknowable name of God. No man can know God. Finite as we are, restricted as we are, the essential deity of God is something a man cannot enter into. It is the very Lord God who is coming, for Christ Jesus is God of this universe. We are not going to see three Gods in heaven. Never persuade yourself that in glory we are going to look at God No. 1 and God No. 2 and God No. 3. No! There is one great Lord God. We know Him as our Father, we know Him as our Savior, we know Him as the Holy Spirit in our hearts. There is one God and this is the great God, called in the Old Testament, Jehovah, and, incarnate, called in the New Testament Jesus, the Prince of heaven, who is coming. "And he was clothed with a vesture dipped in blood [that is the blood of His enemies] . . . and he treadeth the winepress of the fierceness and wrath of Almighty God [against His enemies]."

We read again, ". . . and his name is called The Word of God." This is His pronounceable name; this is His communicable name; this is the name by which we who are mortal know Him. "In the beginning was the Word and the Word was with God and the Word was God" (John 1:1). He became incarnate and we saw His glory as the glory of the only begotten of the Father, full of grace and truth. This is "The Word of God," the Lord Jesus Christ.

We read again: "And out of his mouth goeth a sharp sword, that with it he should smite the nations." He does not need to strike. He speaks and the thing is done. There is illimitable power even in His voice. For example, in the days of His humility, in the days when He was condemned and rejected of men, evil men came to arrest Him. The Lord asked, "Whom do ye seek?" And they said, "Jesus of Nazareth." He said, "I am he." And they all fell to the ground. Even in the days of His humility, the armed guard of the Romans and of the Sanhedrin and of the temple could not stand in His presence. If it was thus in the days of His sorrow, think what it will be when He comes in glory with the hosts of heaven! What power! What strength! The scene is indescribable.

We read again, ". . . and he shall rule them with a rod of iron: and he treadeth the winepress of the fierceness and wrath of Almighty God." This is the day of judgment. "And he hath on his vesture and on his thigh a name written, King of Kings, and Lord of Lords." King of kings and Lord of lords. When the Magi came from the East, they said, "Where is he that is born king?" When Pilate crucified Him and nailed Him to a tree, they put an inscription above Him, saying, "This is Jesus of Nazareth, a *king.*" Whether He is born in a manger or whether He is nailed to a cross or whether He is coming in power with the clouds of heaven, He is a King. *He is a King!*

The Revelation also describes the saints that come with Him: "And the armies which were in heaven followed him upon white horses clothed in fine linen, white and clean." We have already been introduced to these saints in Revelation 19:8. The white linen in which they are clothed is the righteousness of the saints. God's tried, chosen, and faithful people follow their Lord out of heaven. But how did these saints get up there in heaven? Here is another illustration of the fact that, when you interpret this Bible correctly, every little incident or detail will fit. You see, in the fourth chapter of the Revelation, the Church, God's sainted people, are all taken up to glory. Here in chapter 19 when the Lord Jesus comes, these glorious ones, these shining ones, come with Him, having already been up there with Him. Here they come with Him out of the bursting gates of heaven.

The Seer now describes the armies that are warning against the Lord Christ. This is the most unbelievable development in the earth. These who oppose God and oppose His Christ and oppose His Church and oppose His truth, who are they? "And I saw the beast, and the kings of the earth . . . and the false prophet." This trio is leading the blasphemous opposition to the Lord God. In Revelation 13, listen to the boast of the unbelieving as they speak of the invincibility and the immortality of the beast: "And his deadly wound was healed: and all the world wondered after the beast. And they worshipped the dragon which gave power unto the beast: and they worshipped the beast, saying, Who is like unto the beast? who is able to make war with him?" They boast: "We have an invincible and an immortal leader. Look at him! Our great Fuhrer. Our great Il Duce. Our great Commander-in-chief. Look at him, look at him!" And the whole world will wonder after him and worship him. We get a little inkling of that in history. Think of a people adoring a murderer like Hitler. Think of a people adoring a reprobate like Mussolini! Think of a people who have to go through a revolution just to dethrone the memory of a bloodthirsty tyrant like Stalin! All of these things are earnests, types, harbingers, portents, pictures of that awful, ultimate, final tyrant who will come and say: "I can deliver the world. Look at me! Look at me!" And the world follows him.

By the side of the beast is the false prophet. He knows everything. He has all of the answers. He is infallible. There they are, the beast and the false prophet and the dupes who follow them. They are the product of godless government and godless religion. There they stand, all together. You just put this down as an axiom in human history: When a people, when a nation turns aside from the truth and from obedience to the mandates of God, they turn to the most unimaginable oppressions that the mind can think of. They do not turn from God and the Word of God and the blessed Christ into other great truths and into other great revelations and into other great moral and spiritual obediences. They turn to oppression and to all things evil, sordid, damning and terrible.

There is no exception to that axiom in history. Look at it today. Anywhere you find a govenment that repudiates God, and a people who say "No" to our Lord, they are in the morass and the miasma of misery. That is where revolution and war come from. We are not going to have any trouble with a great Christian nation or a godly people. These terrible things come out of the evil spirits that find lodging in the hearts of men who repudiate God. This is the beast and false prophet.

THE GATHERING OF THE ARMIES IN PALESTINE

It is astonishing that all of these vast multitudes of armies are in Palestine. How were they brought together? You would not ordinarily find that great concourse of people in any one country. How do they get there? The answer is found in Revelation 16: 13, 14,16: "I saw three unclean spirits like frogs come out of the mouth of the dragon, and out of the mouth of the beast, and out of the mouth of the false prophet. For they are the spirits of devils, working miracles, which go forth unto the kings of the earth and of the whole world, to gather them to the battle of that great day of God Almighty. And he gathered them together in a place called in the Hebrew tongue Armageddon [*har megiddo*] ." That gathering would not ordinarily happen. But when men give themselves to vile rejection, blasphemy and atheism, when men give themselves to that, then they open their hearts to the spirits of evil and to malicious lies of demons. This is the illustration of the truth in Second Thessalonians 2:11: "God shall send them strong delusion [these that reject God] that they should believe a lie." To them a lie is more truth than truth itself and atheism is more real than God Himself. These evil spirits gather these millions and millions together at this great Judgment Day of Almighty God.

Now, let us look upon the invincible warrior, Christ, and His triumphant victory. The war is over instantly. Is not that a strange thing? You would think, "What power these men have, and these great nations, what power they have!" Against God, they have no might at all. One angel from the Lord, just one, brought to the vast camp of the Assyrians destruction and death when Sennacherib came against the people of Jehovah. Before the terrible power of the Assyrians, Hezekiah the king went down on his face, crying to

God for help. The Lord listened and said, "I see your tears falling on the pavement of the temple and I hear your prayers." Then God sent just one angel, one. When Sennacherib woke up the next morning, as far as his eyes could see there were thousands and thousands and thousands of corpses that once comprised his proud army. Just one angel! Do not ever be persuaded that God who lives in heaven and who looks down upon this earth is about to be overcome. "He that sitteth in the heavens shall laugh: the Lord shall have them in derision." These little Napoleonic crackpots saying big things against God . . . . "He that sitteth in the heavens shall laugh: the Lord shall have them in derision" (Psalm 2:4).

Look how the battle is fought. The beast was taken. God just went down there and snatched him; He just grabbed him! The Almighty, like a big cat with a mouse, just shook the living daylights out of him! The Lord just grabbed him. It says here: "And the beast was taken, and with him the false prophet." With all of his infallibility, he was taken. The Lord just took him and cast him into the lake burning with fire and brimstone. (Notice that a thousand years later, in Revelation 20, they are still in the lake of fire and brimstone.) That is the way the Lord does. He works quickly, instantly, suddenly, with blasphemers and unbelievers. He has always done that. In the Garden of Eden when the woman fell, God talked to her. He turned to the man and talked to him. But notice that He never asked the serpent anything. He never said anything to him. He just cursed him. There are no extenuating circumstances and there are no mitigating details. It is always thus with God-haters and Christ-rejectors. When an apostate who rejects God stands in the presence of the Lord God Almighty, there is nothing to be said. The 63 judgment is over just like that. It is decisive and final.

John does not see the battle. As he did not see the marriage of the Lamb, so he does not see the battle here. He just sees the angel who stands in the sun, stationed in glory, calling for the fowls and the birds of the heavens to come. That is all John sees. The actual war itself and the way it is fought he does not see. But he sees that angel with that awful, awesome announcement. The vultures of the earth come when the earth is bathed in blood. There are only three places in the Bible where that word translated here "fowl" or "bird" is used — in Revelation 18:2 and twice here, once in verse 17 and once in verse 21. These are the only places you will find that word *arnin*. I suppose it refers to "vultures." The angel calls the carrion-eating birds of the earth to come to eat the great men who thought they were bigger than God. They are the wise ones who thought they knew more than God and they are the apostates who rejected the very idea of God. There they are, food for the buzzards, carrion for the vultures. This is the end of those who refuse our great Lord.

We close with Psalm 2, a picture of today: "Why do the heathen rage, and the people imagine a vain thing? The kings of the earth set themselves, and the rulers take counsel together, against the Lord, and against his anointed?" The word in Hebrew for "anointed" is "Messiah." When translated into Greek, it is "Christ." These apostates gather themselves together against the Lord and against His Christ, saying, "Let us do away with them." I once saw a cartoon taken out of a newspaper in Russia. At the bottom of the cartoon were pictures of the churches all broken up. Beyond the rubble of the ruined churches was a ladder leaning against the clouds and there was a workman with a big hammer climbing that ladder to heaven. In heaven was pictured God the Father, God the Son, and God the Holy Spirit. The Soviet workman was taking that hammer and getting ready to bash their brains out. The caption below the cartoon said, "Having destroyed this God business down here in the earth, we are going to destroy it in heaven." What does the Psalm say? "The kings of the earth and the rulers take counsel against his anointed saying, Let us cast them out." But, "He that sitteth in the heavens shall laugh; the Lord shall have them in derision." Oh, the humor of God, the laughter of God! "Then shall he speak unto them in his wrath, and vex them in his sore displeasure . . . I have set my king upon my holy hill of Zion."

An irrefutable, invincible, immovable, unchangeable decree of God is this: Christ shall reign over this whole earth and over all the hosts of heaven. "Thou shalt break them with a rod of iron; thou shalt dash them in pieces like a potter's vessel." The psalmist then makes appeal: "Be wise now therefore, O ye kings: be instructed, ye judges of the earth. Serve the Lord with fear, and rejoice with trembling. Kiss the Son, lest he be angry, and ye perish from the way, when his wrath is kindled but a little. Blessed are all they that put their trust in him."

It is no light thing when a man says "No" to God. It is no triviality, it is no minutia when a man faces the judgment of the Lord God Almighty. All ye judges and ye kings and ye souls in the earth, kiss the Son, bow down before Him, love the Lord Jesus, trust in Him. Blessed are all they that commit their souls' destiny to the Lord Christ.

*This chapter is taken from *Expository Sermons on Revelation*, Vol. 5, by Dr. W.A. Criswell, copyright © 1966 by Zondervan Publishing House. Used by permission.

I HAVE A HOPE

6.

I HAVE A HOPE
PAT BOONE

There is an unforgettable statement from the French historian, Ernest Renan: "All history is incomprehensible without Christ." I have recently come to see the great truth of this.

The events of men and of nations take on significance only in the light of Christ. More than ever, I have seen my own life come to have meaning only by the application of Jesus Christ. Jesus has even given meaning to the frustrating, incomprehensible ups and downs of life. He has answered in my life what I am sure is the basic longing of every man: to know that one's daily affairs are ordered and significant. Suddenly He has moved all things into place, making everything clear.

Christ has done the same thing for human history. Through the years He has been moving everything into place. All history is now clear. Russia is now in her place. Israel is in her place. So are Europe and China.

Our country, like it or not, is moving into its place. The Jesus movement among our young was prophesied long ago in God's Word. Despite the movement's weaknesses, it was ordained in God's history. And I am thankful for it. It is thrilling to see thousands of youth buying Bibles instead of sex magazines. Their preaching, good or bad, is a thousand times more pleasing than having them drop acid or tear up our campuses. Personally, I have thrilled to the great response we have received from our movie, "The Cross and the Switchblade." Such a response would have been unthinkable just four years ago. But now God is fulfilling prophecy and pouring out His Spirit upon our youth.

The miracle of God's Spirit is being experienced in every area of society I know. My business acquaintances, actor and actress associates, laymen and minister friends — so many of them are finding a new dimension in the Holy Spirit. Long ago, God's Word said this would occur in the last days.

The people of our land unfortunately are following another prophecy — they are delving into the occult. I must frankly admit that witchcraft and drug-induced black arts are now big things among Hollywood's jetset. This movement is spreading rapidly, pushing its followers toward their place in history.

When I see these things taking place, when I see the religious and political foundations being laid for Antichrist himself, history suddenly becomes very clear to me. I have a hope which is only strengthened by these frightening events. I believe Jesus Christ is coming back for His people very soon!

The fascinating truth is that this event is destined to be experienced by my generation. Those who live in the Lord *never* see each other for the last time! Only when I discovered this truth did I really begin to live.

If my hope seems absurd to you, it may be that you are the big loser, not me. I like to remember the lines of that *great* grandfather of theatre, Goethe, "Those who hope for no other life are dead even for this."

I pray that you too will come alive in Christ — and
share with me the hope of His return.

PROPHECY
THROUGH THE AGES

PROPHECY
THROUGH THE AGES

600 B.C.: Travel and knowledge explosion of last days.

". . . shut up the words and seal the book, even to the end of time: many shall run to and fro and knowledge shall be increased."

Daniel 12:4

A.D. 65: The "new morality" of the last days.

"You must face the fact: the final age of this world is to be a time of troubles. Men will love nothing but money and self; they will be arrogant, boastful, and abusive; with no respect for parents."

Paul, in 2 Timothy 3:1,2 New English Bible

A.D. 1555: The horror of modern warfare, especially bombs.

"Live fire will be put in globes, hidden death, Horrible, frightful. By night the fleet will reduce the city to rubble, The city on fire, the enemy indulgent."
The French Prophet,

Nostradamus (5.8)

A.D. 1669: The rebuilding of Israel

"When once God shall begin this work of Israel's salvation, it shall be carried on with speed and irresistible might . . . All motions, when they come near their center, are most swift . . . The Israelites, at their return, shall even fly."

*Increase Mather,
President of Harvard College* 73

A.D. 1710: Last days prophecy believers.

"About the Time of the End, a body of men will be raised up who will turn to the Prophecies, and insist upon their literal interpretations, in the midst of much clamor and opposition."

Sir Isaac Newton

A.D. 1800: The Middle-East conflicts of today.

"The nations round them (the Israelis) will make a general combination against them when they least expect it and will gather a numerous and very formidable host to effect their destruction. In this they shall not finally succeed."

*Clergyman and writer,
Dr. Elhanan Winchester*

A.D. 1869: Breaking down of the atom.

"In one hundred years of physical and chemical science, man will know what the atom is. It is our belief that when science reaches this stage, God will come down to earth with his big ring of keys and say to humanity, 'Gentlemen, it is closing time.'"

French chemist *Pierce Berthelot*

A.D. 1921: Destruction of social orders, anarchy, Jewish atrocities, apathy, the "silent majority," and violence.

Things fall apart: the center cannot hold; mere anarchy is loosed upon the world, the blood-dimmed tide is loosed and everywhere the ceremony of innocence* is drowned; The best lack all conviction, while the worst are full of passionate intensity. Surely some revelation is at hand; surely the Second Coming is at hand.

W. B. Yeats

Nobel Prize recipient, poet, and prophet

A.D. 1937: Godless technology's spoilation of the environment.

"Technology is the power with which the earth grips man and subdues him. And because we rule no more, we lose the ground and then the earth is no longer *our* earth, and we become strangers on earth . . . Without God, without his brother, man loses the earth."

Dietrich Bonhoeffer,
who was later executed by the Nazis

*Hitler's slaughter of innocent Jews repeated Herod's slaughter of the innocents in Jesus's day.

A.D. 1967: Anarchy and futility of our time.

"Not only war, famine, pestilence, and revolution, but a legion of other calamities are rampant over the whole world. All values are unsettled; all norms are broken. Mental, moral, aesthetic, and social anarchy reigns."

Dr. Pitirum Sorokin,
Harvard sociologist

TODAY: Need for an experience with God.

"We have turned to conquest of a material nature, and therefore have become very rich in the material sense. But we are poor spiritually. I think it may be time to turn back in that direction, towards religion. I don't mean going to church and reciting certain creeds, the outward form of religion . . . By religion, I mean the inward spiritual form of religion."

Arnold Toynbee, Historian

TODAY: Hunger for God.

"There is a spiritual or religious hunger among young people which standard brand religions just don't satisfy. For one thing, the standard brand religions . . . are not sources of power. This generation wants to experience. It longs for power."

Allen Watts, one of the
founders of the
Flower Movement

TODAY: "Show us Jesus."

"To the church world . . . to all Christians everywhere, here is what we're saying: Don't tell us what you believe. Show us how much like Jesus you are!"

From a baptismal address at
Corona del Mar Beach,
California, where 800 Jesus
people were baptized.

7.

wish we'd all been ready
HERE'S HOW

7.

wish we'd all been ready
HERE'S HOW

Admit it! You are a rebel against God's rulership in your life. You live only to suit yourself. You go your own way, a stubborn, lonely, rebellious sinner. You are not ready for the coming of Christ.

Do you really understand what sin is? Sin is a refusal to live intelligently, to conform your life to the truth of God's Word. It is *not* just a weakness, but a state of rebellion: because you refuse to recognize your very clear obligations to God and man. God honestly wants to give you mercy, pardon, peace, and happiness — but you must accept them on HIS terms.

As a rebel, you have a crippled conscience. The apostle Paul describes it as a "mind and conscience that is defiled" (Titus 1:15). Your conscience was designed by God and given to you for the purpose of evaluating your conduct. It "smiles" when your conduct is right, but "frowns" when it is wrong. God intends for it to be an instrument of blessing to bring tranquility and inner composure. But sin in your life tampers with that tender conscience, leaving it filled with gloom and fear. Christ's salvation marvelously heals the crippled conscience.

Yes, without Christ you are a lonely rebel who does not deserve pity. You have a will, therefore you are responsible for your own sin. There is no such thing as a "helpless sinner."

Do you think it is an accident that this message was delivered to you? Do you think God is not concerned about how you live and how you think? Put that out of your mind! All the forces of heaven are calling to you. You are under the influence of the "outpouring of the Holy Ghost." You must face an hour of truth!

When the disciples asked the Lord, "Who then can be saved?" Jesus answered, "With men it is impossible, but not with God: for with God all things are possible" (Mark 10:26-27). Salvation is a cooperative effort. God initiates the action, and you react. No man is *ever* convicted and converted accidentally! There are powerful, unseen forces at work calling you to repent.

The Holy Spirit fights for your soul, showing you how awful your sin really is. The Word of God pulls at your heart showing you the "goodness of God that leads to repentance." When the message from God's Word gets through to you, it hits you hard — like a hammer breaking a heart of stone. It brings powerful Holy Ghost conviction upon you and exposes all hidden sin in your life.

God also uses friends to lead you to Christ. A true friend will talk to you about the tender compassion of a loving Savior, the joy of heaven, the wrath of God, the terror of hell.

All these ways God uses to change your good intentions into an act of true repentance. *For salvation doesn't really count until you truly repent!*

"Joy shall be in heaven over one sinner that repenteth" (Luke 15:7). Repentance must be your very own act. God uses forces to draw you, but He never forces you to do anything. You alone can turn the rudder of the "ship of life" into the calm waters of obedience. Listen, your salvation hinges on one thing: will you turn from sin? Or not? Salvation without true repentance is absolutely impossible.

True repentance begins with a revelation and an admission of *personal* guilt. You cannot blame anyone else: parents or environment. You must feel your guilt: admit that you are in darkness, condemned, and unable to save yourself. Have you honestly faced the facts? "I am a guilty sinner. I am lost. I am grieving God. I am living only for myself. God, I am sorry." This is what you must do!

Repentance means to completely revolutionize your mind concerning God, self, sin, and your will. God is waiting to see how honest your repentance will be. When you pray "Lord, I repent," you are actually promising "Lord, I am changing my mind about everything. I see what sin does to me. I am tired of selfish living, and I surrender my will to you. Crush my own ambitions and put within me a new heart."

Repentance is a *complete turn away* from being a rebel, from ungodly friends, from secret sins and habits, from filthy books, dirty stories, unclean jokes, from unintelligent living, from wasting time, from anything and anybody that will hinder your being a 100% follower of Christ.

Yes, "I repent" is much more than two little words said under the influence of an emotional experience. It is a declaration of new allegiance, a submission, a pledge to denounce the world once and for all. Christ must become your commander-in-chief. Stop being a little god to yourself. Surrender your sword of bitterness, raise your flag of surrender, and put your life under new management.

No salvation can take place without a very important step being taken to walk in the path of holiness: FAITH! *Faith is the power that continues your conversion.* A great number of passages in the Bible 81 make it very plain that the benefits of salvation become effective only by faith.

IMPORTANT: Faith is not a mere intellectual state of belief. It *is* a complete committal of the will and a full trust and confidence that our sins are forever forgiven by the sacrificial sufferings of Christ on the cross.

Wherever Jesus preached repentance, He preached faith as a follow-up. Mark 1:15, "Repent ye, and *believe* the gospel." John 6:47,48, "He that *believeth* on me hath everlasting life. I am that bread of life."

This faith I am talking about requires deep thinking. Your mind can't drift along in neutral with hopes based on nothing more than happy feelings or "joy pop" religion. Your faith will shift into gear only as you feed on the Word of God and understand what it promises.

Some converts revert to the old life of fear and doubt, then pathetically cry, "I didn't get anything; I don't feel anything," because they did not possess faith. They did not want to "strain" their minds, so they decided their salvation didn't take.

You must reinforce your faith with Bible truth. Once and for all decide, "God said it *so* I believe it *and* that settles it!"

life
on the edge
of time

life
on the edge
of time

Life is now a base camp on the edge of time,
   a platform for mounting expeditions
                        into the origins of existence.
To learn how "to be born again"
   one assumes the possibility of getting lost
                     without becoming a casualty.
But the stresses of the sixties changed all that
   when young people began to eat
                 the fruit of drugs and revolution.

Perhaps it started when the Kennedy laughter was cut off
   by bullets: when our nation became expert
               at staging State funerals.
The summer of love was replaced by the winter of "speed."
   Original hippies of "Haight" disappeared
               into the desert!
Teenyboppers began looking
   for holes to hide in.
               Splitting and shivering became
               epidemic.

     "For those who walk in darkness
   Both in the day time and in the night time
   The right time and right place are not here."
      — T.S. Eliot

They went to the Indian to learn how to live off the land;
 communes sprang up like emergency wards
                    for emaciated victims!
They were saying it with flowers, but no one knew
                    they were funeral flowers!
Life became boring, ugly, senseless.
  Death seemed so satisfying;
                    pontifical and symbolic rhetoric
                    replaced wisdom.
A new left developed,
  Baited by Herbert Marcuse and his Marxist
  theory,

                    They flocked to hear
                    "CAPITALISM IS COLLAPSING!"
The most wanted high school radicals
  sporting around in wire-wheeled Triumphs
                    and silky puff-sleeved shirts
                    experienced political orgasms
                    with revolutionary vibrations.

      "Caught in that sensual music, all neglect
        Monuments of unaging intellect."
— Prophet and 1923 Nobel Prize recipient, W.B. Yeats

But the new revolutionary is anti-intellectual,
  burning libraries
                    and boycotting classes.
The new left prefers the thrill of activist phrases

  Like — "UNDERMINE THE FOUNDATIONS OF THE
  SYSTEM"

                    and "LIBERATE ALL
                    INSTINCTUAL NEEDS" —
Proof enough of the failure of the philosophers
  To the right and left
                    who have done little more than
                    repeat what has already been said!

> "Songs, chants, and slogans of the Slavic people
> While princes and Lord are captive in the prisons
> In the future, by idiots without heads
> Will be received as divine oracles."
> — Nostradamus the prophet, 1555

But this is not the time to die.
  It is time to live
                    and only in Him is the source of life:
JESUS CHRIST — SOLID ROCK!

  He bridges the gap between time and eternity
                    revealing the secret all men now
                    seek:
                    "How to be born again."
Getting into Him makes it happen.
  Man becomes a new creation.
                    The old man with his hang-ups
                    vanishes.
A NEW MAN IS BORN —
  timeless and eternal —
                    who will never die!
Revolution is transitory and weak.
  Jesus Christ brings restoration:
                    Something no revolution has
                    ever done.
Initiation into the restoration movement is only by death —
  to self, to pride, to sin,
                    to the world.
Total realization and eternal freedom is the reward.
  Answer that — if you can,
                    Herbert Marcuse!

> "About the Time of the End, a body of men will be raised up
> who will turn to the Prophecies, and insist upon their literal
> interpretations, in the midst of much clamor and opposition."
> — Sir Isaac Newton, 300 years ago

8.

THE WAY IT WILL BE

8.

THE WAY IT WILL BE

Then I saw an angel descending from heaven, holding in his hand the key of the abyss and an enormous chain. ²He seized the dragon, the serpent of old, who is the devil and Satan, and bound him for a thousand years. ³He hurled him into the abyss, which he shut and sealed above him, that he might lead astray the nations no more until the thousand years are completed. After that he must be released for a little while.

⁴Then I saw thrones that were occupied by such as received power to judge. I also saw the souls of those who had been slain for their testimony to Jesus and for God's message, and of those who had not worshiped either the beast or his statue, nor had received his mark on their foreheads or on their hands. They came to life and reigned with Christ a thousand years.

⁵The rest of the dead did not come to life until the thousand years were completed. This is the first resurrection. ⁶Blessed and holy is he who shares in the first resurrection. Over them the second death exerts no power; instead, they will be priests of God and of Christ, and will reign with Him a thousand years.

⁷When the thousand years have ended, Satan will be released from his prison ⁸and will go out to lead astray the nations in the four quarters of the earth, Gog and Magog, to muster them for battle. Their number is as the sand of the seashore.

⁹They marched up over the breadth of the earth and surrounded the encampment of the saints and the beloved city. And fire came down from heaven and consumed them. ¹⁰The devil, who had deceived them, was flung into the lake of fire and sulphur where also the beast and the false prophet were and they will be tortured day and night forever and ever.

¹¹Then I saw a great white throne and One seated upon it, from whose presence earth and heaven fled, and no room was found for them. ¹²I also saw the dead, great and small, standing before the throne, and scrolls were opened. Another scroll was opened, the Book of Life, and the dead were judged according to their conduct from the entries in the scrolls. ¹³The sea also gave up the dead persons it contained, and death and Hades gave up the dead in them, and each person was judged according to his works. ¹⁴Then were death and Hades hurled into the lake of fire. This is the second death — the lake of fire. ¹⁵And whoever was not found recorded in the Book of Life was cast into the lake of fire.

Then I saw a new heaven and a new earth; for the first heaven and the first earth had passed away, and no longer was there any sea. ²I also saw the holy city, the new Jerusalem, descending out of heaven from God, made ready as a bride adorned for her husband. ³And I heard a loud voice from the throne say, "Behold, God's dwelling place is among men, and He will dwell with them; they shall be his people, and God Himself will be with them ⁴and shall wipe away every tear from their eyes. Death shall be no longer, nor mourning, nor crying, nor any further pain, because the former things have passed away."

⁵Then He who was seated upon the throne said, "Behold, I make all things new." He also said, "Write; for these words are trustworthy and true." ⁶And He

told me, "It is done! I am the Alpha and the Omega, the Beginning and the End. To him who is thirsty, I will give him without charge from the fountain of the water of life. 7The victor shall inherit all this; I shall be his God and he shall be My son....

15The one talking with me had a golden measuring rod to measure the city with its gates and its wall. 16The city is laid out as a quadrangle, with its length equal to its width. With the rod he measured the city, about fifteen hundred miles — the length, the width and the height exactly equal. 17He measured its wall too, two hundred sixteen feet by human measure, that is, by the angel's.

18Its wall was made of jasper, and the city was made of pure gold, as transparent as glass. 19The foundation stones of the city wall were ornamented with every kind of precious stone: the first foundation stone was jasper; the second, sapphire; the third, agate; the fourth, emerald; 20the fifth, sardonyx; the sixth, sardius; the seventh, chrysolite; the eighth, beryl; the ninth, topaz; the tenth, chrysoprase; the eleventh, jacinth; and the twelfth, amethyst.

21The twelve gates were twelve pearls, each separate gate made of one pearl, and the street of the city was made of pure gold, as transparent as glass. 22I saw no temple in it, for the Lord God Omnipotent is its temple, and so is the Lamb. 23The city has no need of the sun or of the moon to shine on it, because God's glory illumines it and the Lamb is its light. 24By its light the nations will walk and to it the kings of the earth will bring their splendor. 25Its gates shall not at all be closed during the day, for there will be no night there. 26Into it they will carry the glory and the honor of the nations. 27But nothing unclean nor anyone practicing immorality and falsehood shall ever enter it, but only those whose names have been recorded in the Lamb's Book of Life.

He then showed me the river of the water of life, as clear as crystal, flowing forth from the throne of God and of the Lamb, ²and running through the middle of the street, and on this side and that side of the river, the tree of life, bearing twelve kinds of fruit, yielding its fruit every month. And the leaves of the tree are for the healing of the nations.

³There shall no longer be anything accursed there, but the throne of God and of the Lamb shall be in it, and His servants shall worship Him. ⁴They shall look at His face and His name shall be on their foreheads. ⁵And night shall be no more; they will need neither lamplight nor sunlight, for the Lord God will be their light, and they shall reign forever and ever.

⁶Then he said to me, "These words are trustworthy and true. The Lord, the God of the spirits of the prophets has sent His angel to show His servants what must shortly take place. ⁷Behold, I come quickly." Blessed is he who observes the words of the prophecy of this book.

⁸I, John, am the one who saw and heard these things, and when I had heard and seen, I bowed down to worship at the feet of the angel who was showing me all this. ⁹But he said to me, "You must not do that! I am a fellow servant of yours, and of your brothers the prophets, and of those who obey the messages of this book. Worship God."

¹⁰Then he said to me, "Do not seal up the words of the prophecy of this book, for the time is near. ¹¹Let him who does wrong do wrong still, and let the filthy still be filthy; let the righteous still do right, and let the saint still be holy."

¹²"Behold, I am coming soon and My reward is with Me, to render to each according to his doings. ¹³I am the Alpha and the Omega, the First and the Last, the Beginning and the End. ¹⁴Blessed are those

who wash their robes, that they have the right to the tree of life and to enter through the gates into the city. ¹⁵Outside are dogs, sorcerers, immoral persons, idolaters, and everyone who loves and practices falsehood.

¹⁶" I, Jesus, have sent My angel to you to witness these things for the churches. I am the Root and the Offspring of David, the brilliant Morning Star."

¹⁷The Spirit and the bride say, "Come!" And let him who hears say, "Come!" And let the thirsty come; he who desires it, let him take freely the water of life.

¹⁸I warn everyone who hears the words of the prophecy of this book: if anyone adds to them, God will add to him the plagues that are described in this book, ¹⁹and if anyone takes away from the words of this prophetic book, God will take away his share in the tree of life and in the holy city as described in this book.

²⁰He who affirms this says, "Yes, I am coming very soon."

Amen, Come, Lord Jesus!

²¹The grace of the Lord Jesus Christ be with all.

(Revelation 20:1-21:7; 21:15-22:21)